CLASSIC ADVERTISING

ARRANGED FOR INTERMEDIATE PIANO
BY JERRY LANNING

Chester Music
(A division of Music Sales Limited)
8/9 Frith Street
London W1V 5TZ

This book © Copyright 1999 Chester Music.
Order No. CH61616   ISBN 0-7119-7740-2

Cover design by Miranda Harvey
Cover photography by George Taylor
Photograph of sky from Superstock
Music setting by Jerry Lanning
Printed in Great Britain by Printwise (Haverhill) Limited, Suffolk.

CONTENTS

Adagietto

from Symphony No.5 in C♯ Minor

Gustav Mahler

Air On The G String

from Suite No.3, BWV 1068

Johann Sebastian Bach

Adagio For Strings

Samuel Barber

Aquarium
from The Carnival Of The Animals

Camille Saint-Saëns

The Arrival Of The Queen Of Sheba

from Solomon

George Frideric Handel

Canon In D

Johann Pachelbel

Chanson de Matin

Edward Elgar

Dance Of The Reed Flutes

from The Nutcracker

Peter Ilyich Tchaikovsky

Moderato assai

Cello Concerto
First Movement

Edward Elgar

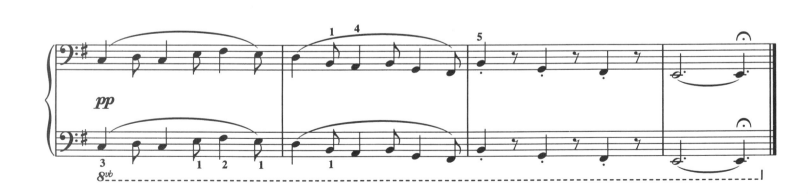

Dies Irae
from the Requiem

Giuseppe Verdi

Allegro agitato

Eine Kleine Nachtmusik

Rondo

Wolfgang Amadeus Mozart

D. 𝄋 al 🔴 Coda (with repeat)   🔴 Coda

The Flower Duet

from Lakmé

Léo Delibes

Jupiter
from The Planets

Andante maestoso

Gustav Holst

Largo
from Symphony No. 9 in E Minor

Antonin Dvořák

Nessun Dorma
from Turandot

Giacomo Puccini

Pavane

Gabriel Fauré

Andante molto moderato

Shepherd's Song

5th Movement from Symphony No.6 in F 'Pastoral'

Ludwig van Beethoven

Toccata in D Minor
BWV 565

Johann Sebastian Bach

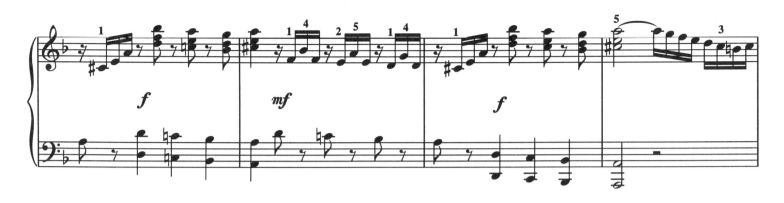

Presto

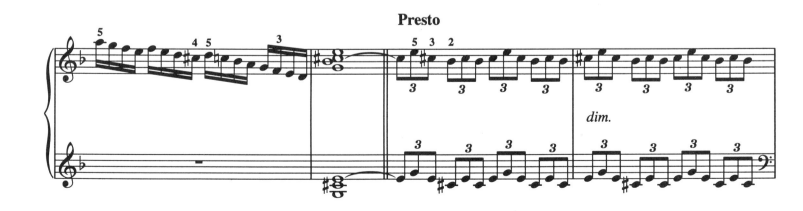

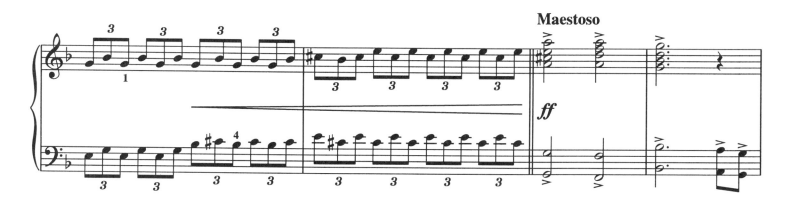

Toreador's Song
from Carmen

Georges Bizet

Vltava

from Ma Vlast

Bedrich Smetana

William Tell Overture

Gioacchino Rossini

1812 Overture

Peter Ilyich Tchaikovsky

Allegro vivace

PIANO MUSIC
AVAILABLE FROM CHESTER MUSIC

CONTEMPORARY CLASSICS
Three collections of masterpieces of the 20th century superbly
arranged for intermediate piano solo. Including works by
Elgar, Ellington, Holst, Sibelius and Stravinsky.
Piano Solo 1 CH61181
Piano Solo 2 CH61182
Piano Duet CH61183

THE GREATEST CLASSICAL MOVIE ALBUM CH61387
Classical masterpieces of the cinema arranged for piano solo:
from *Four Weddings And A Funeral* to *Silence Of The Lambs.*

MANUEL DE FALLA PIANO ALBUM CH61279
Falla's best-known works arranged for intermediate piano solo.
Including works from *El Amor Brujo* and *The Three-Cornered Hat.*

MICHAEL NYMAN
FILM MUSIC FOR SOLO PIANO CH61400
A selection of pieces and arrangements by the composer of his
best-known film music. Including music from *The Draughtsman's
Contract, Drowning By Numbers, Carrington* and *The Piano.*

THE PIANO (Michael Nyman) CH60871
Original compositions for solo piano from the award-winning
film by Jane Campion.

REVISITING THE PIANO (Michael Nyman) CH61411
Four new arrangements available for the first time for solo piano,
plus the two favourite themes from the soundtrack of *The Piano.*

TUNES YOU'VE ALWAYS WANTED TO PLAY CH55834
MORE TUNES YOU'VE ALWAYS WANTED TO PLAY CH58750
DUETS YOU'VE ALWAYS WANTED TO PLAY CH61185
JAZZ TUNES YOU'VE ALWAYS WANTED TO PLAY CH61561
Bumper albums containing classical and traditional favourites
in excellent arrangements for intermediate pianists.

Chester Music
(A division of Music Sales Limited)
Exclusive distributors:
Music Sales Limited, Newmarket Road, Bury St Edmunds, Suffolk IP33 3YB.